ERIC HU

Oh No They DIDN'T

TRAILBLAZERS

Turn the page for some truly wild tales!

ILLUSTRATED BY
SAM CALDWELL

words&pictures

First published in 2025 by words & pictures,
an imprint of The Quarto Group.
100 Cummings Center,
Suite 265D Beverly, MA 01915, USA.
T (978) 282-9590 F (978) 283-2742
www.quarto.com

EEA Representation, WTS Tax d.o.o., Žanova ulica 3, 4000 Kranj, Slovenia

Copyeditor: Nancy Dickmann
Project Editor: Jackie Lui
Designer: Kathryn Davies
Senior Designer: Sarah Chapman-Suire
Creative Director: Malena Stojić
Associate Publisher: Holly Willsher
Production Manager: Nikki Ingram

ISBN: 978-0-7112-9293-2

Printed in Pontian Johor, Malaysia PC052025

9 8 7 6 5 4 3 2 1

ERIC HUANG

Oh No They **DIDN'T**

TRAILBLAZERS

FASCINATING FACTS YOU NEVER KNEW ABOUT AMAZING TRAILBLAZERS!

ILLUSTRATED BY
SAM CALDWELL

words & pictures

CONTENTS

Meet some game-changing champions.

INTRODUCTION

Our lives have been shaped by extraordinary people who've made incredible contributions to the world. Their hard-won achievements have inspired people to pursue their dreams. These trailblazers invented the cutting-edge technology we use every day, as well as common household objects we take for granted. They continue to break barriers, battle for justice, and protect our planet!

Their stories remind us that through determination and compassion, anything is possible. But how much do you really know about these trailblazers?

Everyone knows that **Martin Luther King Jr**. stood up for racial equality. He and his followers used every means possible to fight for civil rights. . . didn't they?

We've all heard of Barbie, the doll created by **Ruth Handler**. Handler set up the toy company Mattel to create Barbie dolls. . . didn't she? And all of them easily persevered in the face of discrimination. . . didn't they?

OH NO THEY DIDN'T!

READ ON to discover what you didn't know about **tremendous trailblazers throughout history.**

Meet musicians who changed the world with their melodies and marine biologists who unveiled the secrets of the deep blue sea.

Dive in!

A dose of knowledge...

We approve.

An adventure through time...

Encounter big bosses who revolutionized industries, and regal royals who led their people with courage.

Learn about the activists who fought tirelessly for justice, the inventors who brought their brilliant ideas to life, and the creators who transformed the world with imagination and ingenuity.

LET'S EXPLORE THE ACHIEVEMENTS OF THESE TRAILBLAZERS!

CHANGEMAKERS
SUPPORTING SUFFRAGE

Trailblazers were responsible for securing women's suffrage, or right to vote. In the early 20th century, British activists invented the word *suffragette* as their name for themselves. . . didn't they?

OH NO THEY DIDN'T!

A male journalist came up with the word. He changed *suffragist*, someone fighting for the right to vote, to *suffragette* as an insult! Instead of taking offense, the activists owned the word and proudly adopted the name.

Emmeline Pankhurst was the trailblazer who led the British suffragettes.

Did you know that her three daughters were also suffragettes? Emmeline and her oldest daughter, **Christabel**, co-founded an activist organization called the Women's Social and Political Union.

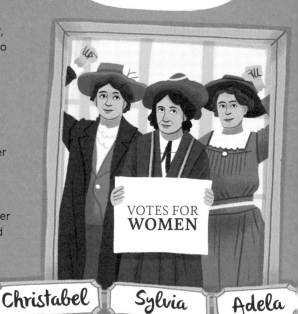

VOTES FOR **WOMEN**

Christabel Sylvia Adela

Never surrender!

Emmeline Pankhurst

The middle daughter, **Sylvia**, formed her own organization—the East London Federation of the Suffragettes—to focus on the rights of working women. **Adela**, the youngest daughter, participated in protests with her family and later moved to Australia. The sisters' bravery led to the passage of laws that granted women the right to vote.

Across the ocean, Susan B. Anthony campaigned for women's suffrage in the U.S. suffrage movement. It was the first movement she was passionate about. . . wasn't it?

OH NO IT WASN'T!

Susan B. Anthony

Slavery was legal in the U.S. during Anthony's lifetime, but she wanted it outlawed. She began working with anti-slavery **abolitionists** when she was only 17!

In 1869, Anthony started the National Woman Suffrage Association with her friend **Elizabeth Cady Stanton**. Their efforts, along with those of many others, eventually led to the Nineteenth Amendment to the U.S. Constitution in 1920, which granted American women the right to vote.

NATIONAL WOMEN SUFFRAGE ASSOCIATION

Progress is the victory of a new thought over old superstitions.

Elizabeth Cady Stanton

Mary Wollstonecraft

Shelley's the spark that brought me to life!

Many suffragists were inspired by the writer **Mary Wollstonecraft.** Her 1792 essay, *A Vindication of the Rights of Woman*, argued that women were equal to men. The work inspired other trailblazers for decades to come.

Did you know that Wollstonecraft's daughter was also a world-famous author? She's **Mary Shelley**, the writer of *Frankenstein!*

CIVIL RIGHTS

Civil rights are personal rights and freedoms that are protected by law. Trailblazers throughout history have championed civil rights for various marginalized groups.

One such trailblazer was **Martin Luther King Jr.** King was a key leader of the U.S. Civil Rights movement in the mid-20th century.

Martin Luther King Jr.

The movement was already underway when a Black woman, **Rosa Parks**, was arrested in Montgomery, Alabama in 1955 for refusing to give up her bus seat to a White man. In protest, King orchestrated a city-wide bus boycott, ultimately leading to the end of segregation on public transportation. Months before Rosa Parks refused to give up her seat, Claudette Colvin, a teenage trailblazer, refused to give up her seat for a White woman as well.

Rosa Parks

King's followers used any means necessary to fight for civil rights. . . didn't they?

OH NO THEY DIDN'T!

King believed in nonviolent action. His peaceful demonstrations and the moving speech he delivered during the March on Washington in 1963 captivated the nation and led to the legal protection of the civil rights of all citizens, regardless of race, socioeconomic status, or religion.

EQUAL RIGHTS NOW!

CIVIL RIGHTS PLUS FULL EMPLOYMENT EQUALS FREEDOM

Ella Baker

The U.S. Civil Rights movement was mainly led by men. . . wasn't it?

OH NO IT WASN'T!

Did you know that Rosa Parks was inspired by Ella Baker? Years before the bus incident, she attended Baker's leadership program. It clearly left a lasting impression—one that would change history!

Women were at the center of the fight! One of the most influential was **Ella Baker**. Like King, Baker believed in peaceful resistance, but she wasn't interested in becoming a public figure. Instead, she fought tirelessly from behind the scenes, organizing training and grassroots campaigns. Among many other achievements, Baker founded the influential civil rights organization, the Student Nonviolent Coordinating Committee (SNCC), which focused on empowering young people and students.

11

PLANET PROTECTORS

Protecting our planet is the mission of trailblazer Sir David Attenborough. The naturalist and broadcaster has amazed generations with documentaries showcasing the diversity of life on Earth. His groundbreaking work has inspired people globally to care about the natural world. Sir David is an animal lover. . . isn't he?

Sir David Attenborough

OH NO HE ISN'T!

Did you know that there are over 40 species named after Sir David Attenborough? This includes quite a few critters you definitely wouldn't cuddle.

Attenborough doesn't consider himself an animal lover! He sees "animal lovers" as people who are only interested in cooing over cute, cuddly creatures like pandas and puppies. He's different because all living things fascinate him—even the creepy-crawlies that few people get sentimental about.

Microleo attenboroughi

Zaglossus attenboroughi

Attenborougharion rubicundus

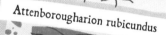

Bindi and Robert Irwin are a planet-protecting double-act who especially love animals many would run from! Together with their mom, these siblings run Australia Zoo, one of the largest conservation facilities in the world. They're passionate about environmental issues and use their celebrity status to rally a new generation of wildlife warriors to save the Earth.

Bindi and Robert Irwin

Did you know that Bindi was named after a crocodile? The animal was rescued by her parents shortly after she was born!

Crikey!

Rachel Carson

Rachel Carson was a trailblazer in marine conservation. She's celebrated today for *Silent Spring*, a book that investigated the harmful effects of pesticides on wildlife, and three books about the oceans. The trilogy explored how the oceans formed, how they worked, and the wondrous creatures that live there. Her work unleashed a surge of interest in protecting the oceans and helped to change environmental protection laws in the U.S.

LGBTQ+ PRIDE

LGBTQ+ Pride is a celebration of queer identities, visibility, and resistance. A leading figure in the fight was Marsha P. Johnson. Johnson was a trans woman and trans-rights activist in New York City who fought against discrimination during the Stonewall Uprising on June 28, 1969. Johnson started the uprising. . . didn't she?

Marsha P. Johnson

OH NO SHE DIDN'T!

Although many applaud Johnson for being the first to fight back when police raided a gay bar called the Stonewall Inn, Johnson said the uprising had already begun when she arrived. Nevertheless, Johnson was one of the most active protesters. Her bravery during the Stonewall Uprising, and activism in the years that followed, motivated queer communities across the world to unite for equal rights.

Did you know that annual Pride events are held in honor of the Stonewall Uprising and trailblazers like Marsha P. Johnson? Most are scheduled in June to commemorate the date of the uprising!

WE'RE **HERE**

WE'RE **QUEER**

EQUAL RIGHTS FOR ALL!

SAY IT *LOUD!* SAY IT *PROUD!*

Shantay, you stay!

At the forefront of today's LGBTQ+ rights movement is the superstar drag queen, **RuPaul**. Her reality show, *RuPaul's Drag Race*, made drag a household word while showcasing a rainbow spectrum of gender expressions.

Empowerment and eleganza!

RuPaul

RuPaul's long time BFF **Michelle Visage** co-hosts *Drag Race*. She was part of the New York ballroom scene, an underground community founded by trans and other queer people of color who competed in pageants called balls. Visage is an ally: a straight person who champions LGBTQ+ rights. Through their trailblazing show, both she and RuPaul have given LGBTQ+ issues a global platform and supported organizations fighting to make inequality sashay away.

Michelle Visage

CREATIVE CATALYSTS LITERARY LEGENDS

William Shakespeare is one of the most quoted writers in history. He wrote nearly 40 plays and 154 sonnets—and introduced hundreds of words and phrases that are still used today! Shakespeare came up with original storylines for classics like *Romeo and Juliet*. . . didn't he?

O Romeo, Romeo! Wherefore art thou Romeo?

OH NO HE DIDN'T!

Many Shakespeare plays were retellings of older stories! The plot of *Romeo and Juliet*, for example, was borrowed from a tale by **Matteo Bandello**.

A play by any other name is still MY play.

William Shakespeare

Shakespeare's words were also borrowed by future writers. **Virginia Woolf** quoted Shakespeare in her novel *Mrs. Dalloway*. He even appears as a character in *Orlando*, another of her novels! Woolf was a trailblazing 20th-century writer. She explored feminist and queer themes, and pioneered stream of consciousness writing, a method of writing whatever comes to mind. Sounds a bit like social media!

Woolf became an exceptional writer after attending the best schools. . . didn't she?

Virginia Woolf

Fear no more the heat o' the sun. . .

OH NO SHE DIDN'T!

In Woolf's time, many girls from well-to-do families were taught at home. Woolf was educated by her parents and developed a love for reading in her family's impressive library.

Another writer who loved reading was **James Baldwin.** As a boy, Baldwin's teachers encouraged his love of stories and took him to an all-Black production of Shakespeare's *Macbeth*. Baldwin would become one of the greatest writers of the 20th century. **Everyone embraced his work. . . didn't they?**

James Baldwin

OH NO THEY DIDN'T!

Baldwin's writing challenged views on race, sexuality, and class. The FBI was so worried about his trailblazing ideas that they spied on him and compiled 1,884 pages of information about his activities! Baldwin wrote profusely, including novels, essays, poems, and plays.

CONFIDENTIAL

17

DISTINGUISHED DANCERS

Julie Felix was the first professional Black ballerina in the UK. When she was 17, she danced in *Sleeping Beauty* with the London Festival Ballet. But Felix wasn't offered a permanent contract with the company because she said no to one. . . didn't she?

> Dancing from Big Ben to the Big Apple.

OH NO SHE DIDN'T!

The ballet company thought Felix was fantastic, but they only wanted White dancers! When Arthur Mitchell, the first Black professional ballet dancer in the U.S., toured in London, Felix auditioned for him and was offered a job. She moved to New York City and toured the world, pirouetting a path for people of color in ballet.

Julie Felix

Alvin Ailey was the founder of the prestigious Alvin Ailey American Dance Theater. Both he and Arthur Mitchell were African Americans who broke barriers for people of color. Like Mitchell, Ailey excelled in ballet. . . didn't he?

OH NO HE DIDN'T!

Alvin Ailey

Alvin Ailey was a master of modern dance. He choreographed elements of ballet into his productions, but also drew inspiration from theater and art forms such as gospel and jazz, which had been pioneered by Black artists. Ailey transformed modern dance while introducing the richness of Black American culture to the world.

Pop star **Shakira** is a dancing queen and one of the most influential Latina women in the world. Of Spanish and Lebanese descent, she mixes Latin and Middle Eastern moves into her performances, igniting global interest in the cultures that influence her.

Did you know that this trailblazer is also a humanitarian? She founded the Barefoot Foundation in her native Colombia to ensure that all children have access to quality education.

Shakira

POP PIONEERS

Hip-hop is a genre of music that was born in the South Bronx area of New York City. New Yorker Lana Michele Moorer is a hip-hop trailblazer better known as MC Lyte. She's the first female rapper to release a full-length solo album. It explores female empowerment, racial inequality, and poverty. Moorer chose the stage name MC Lyte because of its positivity and its similarity to the word "light". She always used MC Lyte when performing. . . didn't she?

OH NO SHE DIDN'T!

MC Lyte's original stage name was Sparkle! It was equally positive, and even though she no longer uses it, the award-winning musician still shines brightly.

Lana Michele Moorer

Never stop sparkling!

Hip-hop has influenced many other musicians, including the K-pop artists **BTS**. BTS is the biggest-selling South Korean act and helped to make K-pop (Korean pop) a global sensation. But the seven members of BTS aren't musicians. **Their record company writes all of their music. . . don't they?**

OH NO THEY DON'T!

Let's pose before we compose.

BTS

BTS members help to write all of their own music. Unlike many K-pop groups, their songs often tackle challenges faced by young people—as well as being bangers you can sing along to at the top of your voice.

BLACKPINK is another world-famous K-pop group. Like BTS, they've broken records with their rap- and hip-hop-inspired music.

BLACKPINK

The members of BLACKPINK are passionate about stopping climate change and use their massive social media presence to urge their fans to get involved.

Both BTS and BLACKPINK are trailblazing acts showcasing Korean music and culture to the world.

PROMINENT PAINTERS

Banksy is a graffiti artist whose spray-painted stenciled works are comments about inequality. The controversial art draws from pop culture to provoke conversations about poverty, war, and politics.

The identity of the artist is top-secret because much of their work appears in public places, often without permission. Recently, fans verified Banksy's identity with photos. . . didn't they?

OH NO THEY DIDN'T!

None of the photos of people in hoodies or caps have been proven to be Banksy. Whoever the artist is, this trailblazer continues to inspire—and outrage.

Banksy?

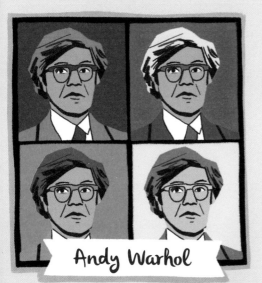

Andy Warhol

Andy Warhol was one of the artists who inspired Banksy. Warhol was obsessed with consumerism and celebrity. As a key figure in the Pop Art movement, which used images from pop culture like cartoons and ads, Warhol challenged the stuffy traditional art world. His most famous works are soup can labels and celebrity portraits. **Andy Warhol only created prints and paintings. . . didn't he?**

OH NO HE DIDN'T!

Warhol was also a filmmaker, writer, and publisher. His art studio, The Factory, was the hippest spot in New York City. It was here that Warhol made many movies and started his magazine, *Interview*, to further explore the concept of celebrity.

One of the many people Warhol interviewed for *Interview* was the iconic painter **Georgia O'Keeffe**, whose most well-known works are paintings of flowers and landscapes. She pioneered techniques to show natural forms as simplified shapes. During her lifetime, O'Keeffe was the most celebrated female American artist. It's no wonder many consider her the mother of American modern art.

Georgia O'Keeffe

AWESOME ATHLETES
SWIFT SPORTSPEOPLE

Sha'Carri Richardson is a track and field record-breaker. She was raised by her grandmother and aunt, who inspired her to become a sprinter. Due to her talent, she effortlessly raced from one triumph to the next. . . didn't she?

OH NO SHE DIDN'T!

Sha'Carri Richardson

Richardson has faced setbacks, such as when she missed out on competing at the 2020 Tokyo Olympics due to a suspension. She has also confronted racism in the sport and criticism of her flashy appearance on the field. Through it all, Richardson remained true to herself and became the fastest woman in the world in 2023!

Olympic champion **Michael Phelps** is one of the fastest swimmers of all time. **Did you know** that he's won more Olympic medals than any other person?

Phelps always looked forward to swimming... didn't he?

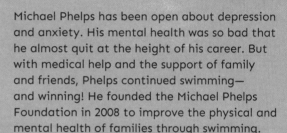

Michael Phelps

OH NO HE DIDN'T!

Michael Phelps has been open about depression and anxiety. His mental health was so bad that he almost quit at the height of his career. But with medical help and the support of family and friends, Phelps continued swimming—and winning! He founded the Michael Phelps Foundation in 2008 to improve the physical and mental health of families through swimming.

Sir Lewis Hamilton

Sir Lewis Hamilton is one of the fastest drivers on the planet. He's the first—and so far, the only—Black Formula One driver. Hamilton set up The Hamilton Commission to find ways of encouraging young Black people to take an interest in motorsports, both behind the wheel as drivers, and under the hood as engineers.

With Hamilton in the lead, a diversity of drivers will be crossing the finish line in the near future!

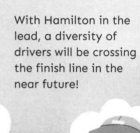

BARRIER BREAKERS

Ade Adepitan is a wheelchair basketball player who won a Paralympic World Cup gold medal in 2005 with the British team. Wheelchair basketball is played in specially designed sports wheelchairs and demands additional skills, such as maneuvering a wheelchair while dribbling the ball!

Did you know that Adepitan is one of the first physically disabled TV hosts in the U.K.? He's also a disability advocate who works with charities to end discrimination.

He shoots. . . he scores!

Ade Adepitan

The awesome athlete **Billie Jean King**, known as BJK for short, has also worked on TV as a tennis commentator. This comes after a stellar career as a professional tennis player, during which she won 39 Grand Slam titles! She also defeated fellow player Bobby Riggs in a special match organized after he boasted that no woman could beat him.

As with many talented athletes, scholarships funded King's training. . . didn't they?

I underestimated her!

OH NO THEY DIDN'T!

Billie Jean King

There were no scholarships for female athletes at King's college! She worked two jobs to support herself. Later in life, she used her fame to fight for women's rights.

She was also the first major female athlete to come out as gay and became an LGBTQ+ sports icon.

Baseball is often called the national pastime of the United States. Jackie Robinson was the first Black Major League Baseball player. . . wasn't he?

Jackie Robinson broke racial barriers—and baseball records—when he played for the Brooklyn Dodgers in 1947. But Moses Fleetwood Walker was the first Black man to play Major League Baseball, all the way back in 1884. Both men had a difficult time, enduring threats, insults, and physical harm. Their perseverance paved the way for future athletes of color, and even inspired Martin Luther King Jr.

OH NO HE WASN'T!

Jackie Robinson

BRILLIANT BALL PLAYERS

Lionel Messi and Cristiano Ronaldo are two of the greatest soccer players of all time. They're trailblazing role models, scoring nearly 2,000 goals between them! Messi and Ronaldo are only trailblazers on the field, though. . . aren't they?

Cristiano Ronaldo

OH NO THEY AREN'T!

Championing children on and off the pitch.

Both are philanthropists! Messi is an ambassador for UNICEF, and Ronaldo has donated more to charities than any other player. Scoring goals and changing lives—Messi and Ronaldo are a double threat!

Lionel Messi

Along with Messi, **Aitana Bonmatí** was named player of the year in 2023 after winning the 2023 World Cup. Bonmatí is passionate about women's rights.

Did you know that she and some of her teammates protested sexism and poor working conditions in the sport? Their actions resulted in changes to improve their well-being, and prompted the Spanish Football Association to drop the word "women" from the title of the sport to demonstrate a new outlook that soccer is soccer, no matter who plays it!

Aitana Bonmatí

Ben Cohen is a champion rugby player who founded the Ben Cohen StandUp Foundation. This anti-bullying organization has supported projects to stop bullying, in particular the bullying of LGBTQ+ young people.

Did you know that Ben Cohen was inducted into the National Gay and Lesbian Sports Hall of Fame? He's been honored many times for his support of LGBTQ+ rights.

Colin Kaepernick is an American football-playing trailblazer. Kaepernick began protesting against racial injustice in the U.S. in 2016 by kneeling during the national anthem. His actions inspired a nationwide debate.

Afterward, Kaepernick's football career skyrocketed. . . didn't it?

OH NO IT DIDN'T!

No professional football team has hired Kaepernick to play for them since the protests. But he's been keeping busy! He founded the Know Your Rights Camp to empower people of color, and he launched Kaepernick Publishing, which publishes books from a diverse range of writers and illustrators.

MIGHTY MEDALISTS

Gymnastics requires strength and skill. The Romanian gymnast Nadia Comăneci had both. She was the first Olympic gymnast to score a perfect 10—and she repeated the record-setting achievement six times! Comăneci always dreamed of being a gymnast. . . didn't she?

Nadia Comăneci

OH NO SHE DIDN'T!

Comăneci was such an active child that her mother enrolled her in gymnastics to tire her out! It didn't work, but the tireless Comăneci became a gymnastics legend.

Simone Biles is another gymnastics legend. She always finds competing easy. . . doesn't she?

OH NO SHE DOESN'T!

Simone Biles

Biles has ADHD, a condition that affects attention and impulse-control. Biles admits that ADHD can make competing very difficult, but it's nothing to be ashamed of. Michael Phelps also has ADHD, and so does champion shot-putter Michelle Carter. Biles is in elite company!

Another mighty medalist was **Siamand Rahman**, the world's strongest Paralympian. Rahman's legs were affected by polio and he used a wheelchair. He took up powerlifting as a teen and set a world record for bench-pressing 683.4 pounds (310 kilograms). That's about the weight of a grand piano! Rahman didn't just have strong arms, he also had immense inner strength.

Siamand Rahman

Strength sports like powerlifting are for men, which means women have always avoided them. . . haven't they?

KATIE SANDWINA

MIRIAM KATE WILLIAMS

OH NO THEY HAVEN'T!

One hundred years ago, pioneering performers known as strongwomen amazed audiences with feats of strength. Three of the most famous were **Katie Sandwina, Miriam Kate Williams** (who performed as "Vulcana"), and **Josephine Blatt** (whose stage name was "Minerva"). Women's weightlifting debuted at the Olympics in the year 2000, with Dika Toua from Papua New Guinea becoming the first woman to lift the sport to new heights.

JOSEPHINE BLATT

EXCEPTIONAL EXPLORERS
DEEP DIVERS

Jacques Cousteau was a trailblazer who explored the seas when he wasn't making award-winning films, inventing diving equipment, and founding the Cousteau Society to protect the oceans. Cousteau always dreamed of a life at sea. . . didn't he?

OH NO HE DIDN'T!

As a young man, Cousteau joined the French navy to become a pilot! But a car accident ended his high-flying dreams. While recovering, he took up swimming in the ocean. It wasn't long before Cousteau was hooked!

Robert Ballard is an oceanographer who pioneered deep-sea exploration using submersibles and remotely operated vehicles. **Did you know** that Ballard and his team discovered the sunken wreckage of the *Titanic* in 1985? **They found the famous ship on behalf of the U.S. Navy. . . didn't they?**

ROBERT BALLARD

OH NO THEY DIDN'T!

The U.S. Navy wasn't interested in the *Titanic*. They gave Ballard money to investigate two sunken submarines. After that, he was free to find the *Titanic*. Since then, Ballard has become a pioneer in marine archeology. He and his team also discovered hydrothermal vents—openings in the ocean floor that spew out superheated water. They're literal hotspots that teem with a unique ecosystem of undersea creatures!

Sylvia Earle

Sylvia Earle is an aquanaut who was inspired by Rachel Carson. In 1970, she lived in an underwater laboratory for two weeks to study the ocean.

Did you know that Earle was the first woman to pilot a submersible? She's led over 50 expeditions and even walked on the ocean floor in a special suit, 1,250 feet (381 meters) below the surface! After her record-breaking ramble, Earle was given a nautical nickname: Her Deepness.

AWESOME ADVENTURERS

Roald Amundsen was the first person to reach the South Pole. He always planned to set this record. . . didn't he?

Roald Amundsen

OH NO HE DIDN'T!

Amundsen originally had his sights set on being first to the North Pole. But while he was raising funds for an expedition, both Frederick Cook and Robert Peary claimed they had reached it. So, Amundsen decided to journey south instead, successfully becoming the first to reach the South Pole in 1911.

You clearly didn't reach the North Pole before I did!

Now's my chance to run for it—and be the first. . .

Fifteen years later, the adventurer finally saw the North Pole. . . from an airship! And because Cook and Peary's claims were never proven, that leaves Amundsen in pole position to be the first person to reach both the North and South Poles.

Nellie Bly was another world traveler. She set a world record by traveling all the way around the world in just 72 days! Bly was a journalist. Her globetrotting trip was accompanied by news stories charting her adventures. But Bly did much more than write travel journals. She began her career reporting on the unsafe conditions faced by female factory workers.

These exposés made Bly a sought-after journalist. . . didn't they?

OH NO THEY DIDN'T!

Nellie Bly

Factory bosses didn't like her articles and convinced Bly's bosses to reassign her to harmless topics like gardening. So Bly carved her own path.

She traveled to Mexico and war-torn Europe as a foreign correspondent and supported the U.S. women's suffrage movement. Most famously, Bly went undercover to investigate an asylum. Her article resulted in the reform of mental health services.

Did you know that Bly was also an inventor? She patented a milk can and also a stackable garbage can. Talk about a can-do attitude!

PEERLESS PIONEERS

Sacagawea trekked with the Lewis and Clark Expedition, exploring the lands between the Mississippi River and the Pacific Ocean from 1804–06. Meriwether Lewis and William Clark hired Sacagawea, a Lemhi Shoshone woman, to be their interpreter with Native Americans they encountered on the journey. . . didn't they?

Sacagawea

OH NO THEY DIDN'T!

Lewis and Clark hired Sacagawea's husband, Toussaint Charbonneau. He brought Sacagawea along—and it was lucky he did! Sacagawea could speak the Shoshone language, which her husband couldn't. She negotiated with Indigenous peoples for horses to cross the Rocky Mountains. She rescued expedition journals when a boat capsized and traded her own beaded belt for a robe to be presented to the U.S. President. Even though Charbonneau got the gig, Sacagawea was the star of the show!

I've always wanted a holiday in the Rockies.

Almost 1,000 years earlier, in the tenth century, the Viking explorer Leif Erikson set foot on what is today eastern Canada. Erikson was the first European to travel to mainland North America. . . wasn't he?

OH NO HE WASN'T!

Leif Erikson

Fellow explorer Bjarni Herjólfsson was probably the first European to see the continent. But Herjólfsson and his crew didn't get off their ship because they were lost—they were trying to reach Greenland.

WELCOME TO GREENLAND

When Erikson reached North America about 15 years later, he became the first European to actually walk on the mainland.

About 1,000 years earlier than that, in the second century, Chinese explorer Zhang Qian explored central Asia. His pioneering journeys resulted in cross-cultural connections between the peoples of modern-day China, India, Iran, and beyond—and they led to the creation of a vast trade network called the Silk Road, stretching from East Asia to Europe!

Zhang Qian

AMAZING ASTRONAUTS

Astronaut Neil Armstrong was the first person to walk on the Moon. This trailblazing achievement was summarized in his famous line, "That's one small step for man, one giant leap for mankind". . . wasn't it?

Neil Armstrong

OH NO IT WASN'T!

The "a" must've taken a leap of its own.

When Armstrong stepped onto the Moon's surface, he actually said, "That's one small step for a man, one giant leap for mankind." But the "a" didn't make it through the radio transmission. Back on Earth, the 650 million people watching the landing live on TV only heard, "That's one small step for man. . ." Hey—no one knew before that day if the signal would be good on the Moon!

Did you know that Armstrong also traveled to the North Pole? He'd already seen the pole from space, but in 1985 he got the chance to see what it would look like up close.

Eight years before Armstrong's moonwalk, cosmonaut Yuri Gagarin became the first person to travel into space. Like Neil Armstrong, who stood 5 feet 11 inches (1.80 meters) tall, Gagarin was a big guy. . . wasn't he?

OH NO HE WASN'T!

Yuri Gagarin

Gagarin was only 5 feet 2 inches (1.57 meters) tall. His small size was a massive advantage! The spacecraft was designed for a pilot shorter than 5 feet 7 inches (1.70 meters).

Armstrong wouldn't have been able to squeeze in, but Gagarin fit the bill perfectly. With his big, winning smile and charming personality, he became a celebrity when he returned to Earth.

Valentina Tereshkova

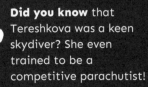

The first woman in space was his fellow cosmonaut, **Valentina Tereshkova**. Gagarin only orbited Earth for 1 hour and 48 minutes during his flight in 1961, but two years later Tereshkova spent three days in space!

Did you know that Tereshkova was a keen skydiver? She even trained to be a competitive parachutist!

LEGENDARY LEADERS
REMARKABLE ROYALS

Lady Diana Spencer was a remarkable royal. Her compassion for AIDS patients, many of whom were gay men, was instrumental in changing discriminatory opinions about people with the disease. Her focus on philanthropy earned her the nickname "the people's princess," but her official title was "Princess Diana". . . wasn't it?

OH NO IT WASN'T!

Lady Diana Spencer

When she married into the British royal family, Diana received the title "Princess of Wales." "Princess Diana" was a nickname from the press. Given her worldwide popularity, the princess was also called the "Queen of Hearts"!

Another champion of the people was Boudicca, a British queen who reigned almost 2,000 years ago. She led her tribe, the Iceni, in a fight against Roman rule.

Did you know that Boudicca's name means "victory"? Although she scored decisive victories against the Romans, she wasn't able to liberate her people. Nevertheless, the ferocity of this warrior queen has made her a trailblazing symbol of resistance and female empowerment.

The first Queen Victoria!

Queen Boudicca

Alexander the Great

Alexander the Great was a warrior king who never lost a battle. His empire was one of the largest ever, stretching from the Mediterranean Sea all the way to South Asia. Alexander's empire connected a vast diversity of cultures and led to the exchange of ideas, foods, and fashions.

This remarkable royal founded more than 20 cities. He named all of them after himself. . . didn't he?

OH NO HE DIDN'T!

I'm the mane event in this city!

The ancient king gave one of the cities a different name: Bucephala. That was the name of his favorite horse, who must've loved the neigh-borhood.

POPULAR POLITICIANS

Abraham Lincoln was one of the most popular U.S. presidents—and not just because of his stylish stovepipe hat and beard. As president, he kept the country together during the American Civil War and ended slavery. Although Lincoln was responsible for outlawing slavery in the U.S., he enslaved people himself. . . didn't he?

OH NO HE DIDN'T!

Although several presidents were enslavers themselves, Abraham Lincoln never was. He described himself as "naturally anti-slavery" and believed it immoral to enslave another human.

Did you know that Abraham Lincoln is the only U.S. president to hold a patent? He invented a device to lift boats over obstacles in the water!

Abraham Lincoln

Sir Winston Churchill was another popular politician who led his country during wartime. Considered one of Britain's greatest prime ministers, Churchill's courage and leadership helped lead his country to victory over the Nazis in the Second World War.

His V-for-victory hand gesture became an international symbol of resistance. He invented the gesture. . . didn't he?

SIR WINSTON CHURCHILL

OH NO HE DIDN'T!

Belgian politician Victor de Laveleye came up with the victory hand gesture. But it was Churchill who made the hand signal world famous.

I'll let you have it, Winnie. . .

Helen Clark was one of New Zealand's most popular prime ministers. She was the first woman to be elected prime minister of the country and served for nine years! Her success in politics paved the way for other female politicians in New Zealand. In 2019, she set up the Helen Clark Foundation to promote inclusion, fairness, and sustainability.

Did you know that Clark was voted Greatest Living New Zealander in an online poll?

Helen Clark

43

HEAD HONCHOS

Many corporate leaders are also trailblazers. Ruth Handler was the president and co-founder of Mattel, the toy company behind the mega-popular Barbie doll. Handler and her husband started the company to make the dolls. . . didn't they?

OH NO THEY DIDN'T!

Mattel was set up to make dollhouse furniture using wood and plastic scraps! The company didn't begin making Barbie dolls until more than ten years later. Handler created Barbie because she saw an opportunity. Most dolls for children were babies. Handler thought an adult doll would capture the imagination of the world. She was right!

Ruth Handler

From bedside tables to Barbie dolls!

Steve Jobs also saw an opportunity when he founded computer company Apple, Inc. with his business partner Steve Wozniak. In 1976, most computers were huge—and hugely expensive. The Apple computer they launched was portable and more affordable.

The business partners became overnight successes. . . didn't they?

OH NO THEY DIDN'T!

Steve Jobs

Only 175 Apple I computers were sold, but they raised enough money to fund the development of the Apple II, the first personal computer with a full-color display. This was the computer that made Jobs and Wozniak mega-successful. As head honcho of Apple, Jobs transformed the computer company into a multimedia tech giant!

Sam Altman

Sam Altman is also revolutionizing tech. His company, OpenAI, is a research lab that develops artificial intelligence to make computers think and learn.

Did you know that Altman is one of a growing number of queer business leaders in tech? He came out when he was 17 years old after defending an LGBTQ+ speaker from bullies at his school.

REVOLUTIONARY REFORMERS

Nelson Mandela was a reformer who helped end apartheid, a system of racial segregation in South Africa. He accomplished this by leading huge rallies. . . didn't he?

OH NO HE DIDN'T!

Nelson Mandela

In the decades leading up to the fall of apartheid, Mandela stopped attending anti-apartheid rallies. But he had a very good excuse: he was serving a 27-year prison term because of his activism. He continued to lead the movement from behind bars and became a global icon.

Upon his release in 1990, Mandela began negotiations to end apartheid. In 1994, he became South Africa's first Black president.

Like Mandela, **Gandhi** was a lawyer. He lived for a time in South Africa where the racism he experienced convinced him to become an activist. Returning to India, Gandhi used nonviolent resistance to help his homeland gain independence from British rule. Nelson Mandela greatly admired Gandhi, as did Martin Luther King Jr., who followed Gandhi's nonviolent methods to make history.

Mahatma is Gandhi's first name. . . isn't it?

OH NO IT ISN'T!

Mahatma, meaning "great soul," is a title given to a highly respected person. Gandhi's actual first name was Mohandas.

Mahatma Gandhi

In the Philippines, Corazon Aquino also led a nonviolent revolution. She became president in 1986 and restored democracy to the island nation. Aquino always wanted to be president. . . didn't she?

OH NO SHE DIDN'T!

Corazon Aquino

Aquino entered politics after her husband was assassinated on the orders of dictator Ferdinand Marcos. She hadn't even planned on running for president until the public convinced her to do so. With support from the Filipino people and members of the government, Aquino defeated Marcos in a peaceful revolution called the People Power Revolution.

INSPIRING INNOVATORS
DNA DECODERS

Gregor Mendel was a scientist who conducted experiments on peas. At the abbey where he lived and worked, he bred plants with different characteristics with each other to study the results. What he discovered became the modern science of genetics, the study of traits that are inherited or passed down from parents to offspring. When Mendel shared his ground-breaking discoveries, scientists applauded his work. . . didn't they?

Gregor Mendel

OH NO THEY DIDN'T!

Mendel's study was given the cold shoulder for about 40 years! It wasn't until 1900 that researchers rediscovered his work. Thanks to his trailblazing contributions to the field, Mendel is celebrated as the father of modern genetics.

I think you're my great-great-grandpea.

We're three peas in a pod.

DNA is the molecule that carries genes, the blueprints for how living things look and behave. **James Watson** and **Francis Crick** are famous for decoding DNA.

They discovered the spiraling double helix structure of DNA through their own experiments and research. . . didn't they?

OH NO THEY DIDN'T!

It was chemist **Rosalind Franklin** who uncovered DNA's spiral shape. Watson attended one of her lectures, and saw an X-ray photograph she had taken of DNA. Franklin's discoveries were critical to Watson and Crick's success, but when they announced their findings, they didn't give her any credit! Luckily, Franklin is now getting the credit she deserves.

Did you know that there are three stage plays and a musical about her life and work? Numerous labs, school, awards, and medical facilities are named after her today. This unsung hero is finally taking center stage!

Rosalind Franklin

MEDICAL MARVELS

Florence Nightingale transformed the medical profession as a trailblazing nurse. She wanted to be a nurse since she was a teenager. Her parents supported her dream. . . didn't they?

Florence Nightingale

OH NO THEY DIDN'T!

Nightingale's parents wanted her to marry, not work. Nightingale chose her own path, though, and studied nursing, then ran a war hospital during the Crimean War. The improvements she made in hygiene and sanitation were soon adopted by other hospitals.

Wash your hands before dinner.

The data shows you're on the fast track to recovery.

Did you know that Nightingale was a gifted statistician? She used statistics to greatly improve hospitals and patient care. Nightingale even invented a new kind of graph, called the Nightingale Rose Diagram!

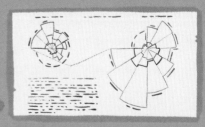

Mary Seacole was a Jamaican nurse who also helped soldiers during the Crimean War. Seacole was rejected from official nursing positions because of racial bias, so she raised money to travel to Crimea herself, where she opened the British Hotel, a restaurant and store for soldiers.

Mary, you're the hostess with the mostest!

Mary Seacole

She used the profits she made to buy medicine to treat the wounded on the battlefield.

Sir Alexander Fleming discovered an antibiotic in 1928, which later saved thousands of lives during the Second World Wae. Fleming conducted a ton of experiments in order to discover penicillin. . . didn't he?

Sir Alexander Fleming

OH NO HE DIDN'T!

En garde, bacteria!

The discovery was accidental! Fleming left a dish of bacteria in his lab while away on vacation. When he returned, a fungus had appeared, killing the bacteria around it.

Scientists then isolated the bacteria-killing chemical in the fungus to create penicillin. So before you wash the dishes, check if they contain the next miracle cure!

TECH TRENDSETTERS

A number of trailblazers are leading a movement to make sure that technological innovation is ethical and a benefit to humankind.

Yoky Matsuoka is an electrical engineer and computer scientist who pioneered a robotic hand capable of mimicking the complex movements of a real human. Her innovation has the potential to help people with hand impairments grasp and manipulate objects.

Matsuoka had an interest in technology since she was young. . . didn't she?

Yoky Matsuoka

OH NO SHE DIDN'T!

Matsuoka trained to become a professional tennis player, but ankle injuries ended her sporting dreams. The setback led to an idea to build a tennis-playing robot, which paved the way to a Grand Slam-worthy career as a scientist who improves people's lives through technology.

Joy Buolamwini and **Fei-Fei Li** are innovators making significant contributions to the ethical development of AI.

Li focuses on developing AI in health care to detect illnesses and create new drugs to fight them. She founded the non-profit AI4ALL to increase diversity and inclusion in the field, which has included AI summer programs for high school girls to foster interest in science and technology.

Li has helped increase the diversity of people working in AI. But AI programming is already inclusive. . . isn't it?

fei-fei Li

OH NO IT ISN'T!

AI uses computer programs called algorithms, and Joy Buolamwini discovered that many AI facial recognition systems couldn't recognize her face because she's Black! The data these AI programs learn from contains biases, leading to biased results.

Joy Buolamwini

In 2016, Buolamwini started the Algorithmic Justice League to raise awareness of potential harms, and partner with companies and governments to address the issues.

INGENIOUS INVENTORS

Ingenious inventors create everyday items we take for granted—like sweatshirts, for example!

The sweatshirt was invented by football player Benjamin Russell Jr. in 1926. Russell was tired of wearing itchy wool pullovers, so he teamed up with his father, a clothing manufacturer, to invent a comfortable cotton alternative. The first sweatshirts often had a V-shaped piece of fabric at the front.

Russell added these because they looked super stylish. . . didn't he?

OH NO HE DIDN'T!

Benjamin Russell Jr.

Pass the ball? No sweat!

The fabric's purpose, like the purpose of the sweatshirt, was to soak up sweat! It's all in the name. The same is true of sweaters, designed for athletes to make them sweat while warming up their muscles before competitions. This means that two of the most popular items of clothing ever are sweat sponges. Delightful!

Bubble tea is a popular drink that's enjoyed around the world. Two people claim to be its inventors. One is Lin Hsiu Hui from Taiwan. She spent years cooking up the recipe. . . didn't she?

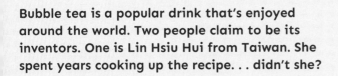

OH NO SHE DIDN'T!

Lin was bored during a meeting and poured a bowl of tapioca dessert into her Assam tea. The result was a tasty, trendsetting treat!

Lin Hsiu Hui

Tu Tsong He

The second alleged inventor was **Tu Tsong He**. Tu was inspired by his childhood love for a smaller, white tapioca and spooned the sweet balls into green tea for an equally delectable drink.

The delicious dispute went to court. After ten years, judges ruled that no matter who invented it, bubble tea couldn't be patented by any one person—paving the way for an international bubble tea frenzy!

TIMELINE

Trailblazing people have been setting trends and breaking the rules for centuries. Travel through time to see when all of the prominent people you've just read about were born.

356 BCE
Alexander the Great

195 BCE
Zhang Qian

1864
Nellie Bly

1858
Emmeline Pankhurst

1822
Gregor Mendel

1869
Mohandas Gandhi

1872
Roald Amundsen

1874
Winston Churchill

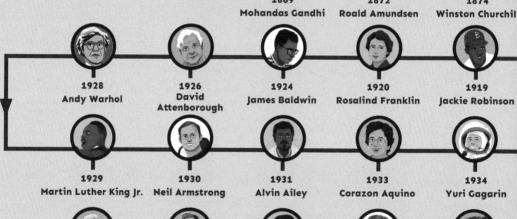

1928
Andy Warhol

1926
David Attenborough

1924
James Baldwin

1920
Rosalind Franklin

1919
Jackie Robinson

1929
Martin Luther King Jr.

1930
Neil Armstrong

1931
Alvin Ailey

1933
Corazon Aquino

1934
Yuri Gagarin

1970
MC Lyte

1968
Michelle Visage

1967
Lin Hsiu Hui

1961
Diana, Princess of Wales

1961
Nadia Comăneci

?
Banksy

1972
Yoky Matsuoka

1973
Ade Adepitan

1976
Fei-Fei Li

1977
Shakira

1978
Ben Cohen

2016
BLACKPINK

2010
BTS

2003
Robert Irwin

2000
Sha'Carri Richardson

1998
Aitana Bonmatí

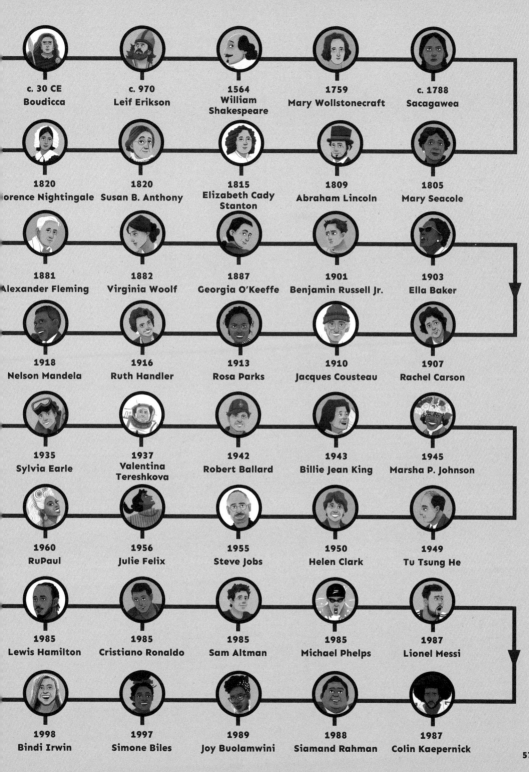

c. 30 CE
Boudicca

c. 970
Leif Erikson

1564
William Shakespeare

1759
Mary Wollstonecraft

c. 1788
Sacagawea

1820
Florence Nightingale

1820
Susan B. Anthony

1815
Elizabeth Cady Stanton

1809
Abraham Lincoln

1805
Mary Seacole

1881
Alexander Fleming

1882
Virginia Woolf

1887
Georgia O'Keeffe

1901
Benjamin Russell Jr.

1903
Ella Baker

1918
Nelson Mandela

1916
Ruth Handler

1913
Rosa Parks

1910
Jacques Cousteau

1907
Rachel Carson

1935
Sylvia Earle

1937
Valentina Tereshkova

1942
Robert Ballard

1943
Billie Jean King

1945
Marsha P. Johnson

1960
RuPaul

1956
Julie Felix

1955
Steve Jobs

1950
Helen Clark

1949
Tu Tsung He

1985
Lewis Hamilton

1985
Cristiano Ronaldo

1985
Sam Altman

1985
Michael Phelps

1987
Lionel Messi

1998
Bindi Irwin

1997
Simone Biles

1989
Joy Buolamwini

1988
Siamand Rahman

1987
Colin Kaepernick

MAP

Have a look at where in the world each of the trailblazers hail from. As you can see, trailblazing is a global effort!

CALIFORNIA, USA

RuPaul
San Diego

Billie Jean King
Long Beach

Steve Jobs
San Francisco

OHIO, USA

Simone Biles
Columbus

Moses Fleetwood Walker
Mount Pleasant

Neil Armstrong
Wapakoneta

Roald Amundsen
Borge, Norway

Leif Erikson
Iceland?

Sacagawea
present-day
Lemhi County, ID

Georgia O'Keeffe
Sun Prairie, WI

Sam Altman
Chicago, IL

Colin Kaepernick
Milwaukee, WI

Robert Ballard
Wichita, KS

Susan B. Anthony
Adams, MA

Alexander Fleming
Darvel, Scotland

Joy Buolamwini
Edmonton, Canada

Ruth Handler
Denver, CO

Cristiano Ronaldo
Funchal, Madeira

Abraham Lincoln
near Hodgenville, KY

Marsha P. Johnson
Elizabeth, NJ

Rachel Carson
Springdale, PA

Sylvia Earle
Gibbstown, Greenwich Township, NJ

Andy Warhol
Pittsburgh, PA

Michelle Visage
Perth Amboy, NJ

Nellie Bly
Cochran's Mills, PA

Michael Phelps
Baltimore, MD

Mary Seacole
Kingston, Jamaica

Jackie Robinson
Cairo, GA

Aitana Bonmatí
Sant Pere de Ribes, Spain

Shakira
Barranquilla, Colombia

SOUTHERN & SOUTHEASTERN USA

Martin Luther King Jr.
Atlanta, GA

Florence Price
Little Rock, AR

Beulah Louise Henry
Raleigh, NC

Alvin Ailey
Rogers, TX

Sha'Carri Richardson
Dallas, TX

Ella Baker
Norfolk, VA

Rosa Parks
Tuskegee, AL

Lionel Messi
Rosario, Argentina

NEW YORK, USA

James Baldwin
New York

MC Lyte
New York

Arthur Mitchell
New York

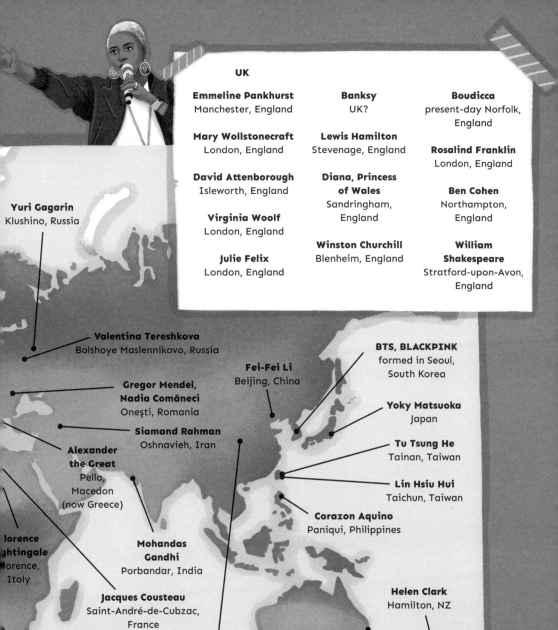

Yuri Gagarin
Klushino, Russia

UK

Emmeline Pankhurst
Manchester, England

Banksy
UK?

Boudicca
present-day Norfolk,
England

Mary Wollstonecraft
London, England

Lewis Hamilton
Stevenage, England

Rosalind Franklin
London, England

David Attenborough
Isleworth, England

**Diana, Princess
of Wales**
Sandringham,
England

Ben Cohen
Northampton,
England

Virginia Woolf
London, England

Julie Felix
London, England

Winston Churchill
Blenheim, England

**William
Shakespeare**
Stratford-upon-Avon,
England

Valentina Tereshkova
Bolshoye Maslennikovo, Russia

Fei-Fei Li
Beijing, China

BTS, BLACKPINK
formed in Seoul,
South Korea

**Gregor Mendel,
Nadia Comăneci**
Oneşti, Romania

Yoky Matsuoka
Japan

Siamand Rahman
Oshnavieh, Iran

Tu Tsung He
Tainan, Taiwan

**Alexander
the Great**
Pella,
Macedon
(now Greece)

Lin Hsiu Hui
Taichun, Taiwan

Corazon Aquino
Paniqui, Philippines

**lorence
ightingale**
lorence,
Italy

**Mohandas
Gandhi**
Porbandar, India

Helen Clark
Hamilton, NZ

Jacques Cousteau
Saint-André-de-Cubzac,
France

Nelson Mandela
Mvezo, South Africa

Zhang Qian
near Hanzhong, China

Ade Adepitan
Lagos, Nigeria

**Robert Irwin,
Bindi Irwin**
Buderim, Australia

GLOSSARY

abolitionist someone who campaigns for an end to slavery

ADHD (short for attention deficit hyperactivity disorder) a mental health condition that can affect attention and behavior

AIDS a disease that weakens the immune system and leaves the body unable to fight off infection and disease

algorithm a set of instructions followed by a computer program

ally a supporter of a person or group, especially a straight person who supports the rights of LGBTQ+ people

amendment a change to an official document, such as the U.S. Constitution

American Civil War a war fought in the United States from 1861–1865, between Northern and Southern states

antibiotic a type of medicine that fights bacteria that cause infection

anxiety a mental health condition that involves feeling extremely worried

apartheid a system of segregation and oppression in South Africa that gave the lowest status to Black people and the highest status to White people; Black people born there were being oppressed in their own homeland

aquanaut a scientist who lives underwater

artificial intelligence (AI) a computer system with programming that allows it to think and learn in the same way as a human brain

asylum a kind of hospital in the past for people with mental illnesses

bias a tendency to favor one group or idea over another

boycott a refusal to buy or support something as a form of protest

civil rights the rights to equal treatment regardless of race, religion, or gender that people have in society, such as the right to vote

climate change change in the Earth's climate caused by human activity

conservation protecting the natural environment

consumerism the idea that it's important to buy and own many things

cosmonaut the Russian term for an astronaut

Crimean War a war fought in the 1850s between the Russian Empire and the United Kingdom and its allies, which took place on the Crimean Peninsula in modern-day Ukraine

depression a mental disorder marked by deep, persistent feelings of sadness and hopelessness

double helix a shape formed by two spring-like spirals, which is the structure of DNA

drag performer someone who uses clothing and makeup to create an exaggerated performance that plays with gender expression

ecosystem the complex, interdependent web made up of the living organisms in a given area and their environment

ethical based on moral principles and aiming to do the right thing

feminist a person who believes that women and people of all or no genders should have the same rights, power, and opportunities as men

graffiti art art created in a public space, often without permission, such as by spray-painting on walls

grassroots coming from the people rather than the government

humanitarian a person who works for the well-being of others

LGBTQ+ an acronym that refers to a wide range of people who are not heterosexual or traditionally male/female

molecule two or more atoms chemically bound together

naturalist a person who studies plants, animals, and other living things

nonviolent resistance activism that involves marches, speeches, and other nonviolent activities

oceanographer a scientist who studies the ocean

patent a legal document that protects a person's or company's right to make and sell an invention

philanthropist a person who donates money to help others

Pop Art an art movement that began in the 1950s which is inspired by everyday objects

Pride a celebration of LGBTQ+ people and culture, with the aim of promoting visibility and equal rights

queer describes sexual and gender identities that are not heterosexual or traditionally male/female

racism the belief that people of some races are inferior, and the practice of treating people differently because of this

Second World War a war fought around the world from 1939–1945, involving many different countries arranged into two alliances

segregation the practice of keeping people apart based on their race, sex, or religion

sonnet a form of poetry that contains fourteen lines arranged in a fixed rhyming pattern

statistician a person who gathers, organizes, and analyzes data

submersible a small vehicle that operates underwater for short periods

suffrage the right to vote

UNICEF (short for United Nations Children's Fund) a charity that provides humanitarian aid to help children around the world

visibility a term used to describe how much people are aware of issues and particular groups

ABOUT THE AUTHOR

Eric Huang was born in New Jersey and grew up in California. He loved mythology, nature, comic books, and more than anything else. . . dinosaurs. When Eric went to college, he studied paleontology, hoping to find fossils. But life took him all the way to Australia, where he found kangaroos and koalas instead. Since then, Eric has worked with Disney, Penguin Books, and LEGO—and found a few fossils along the way. He now teaches at City, University of London, writes books, and makes podcasts.

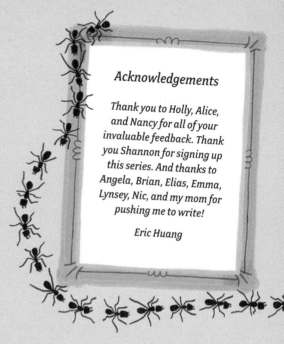

Acknowledgements

Thank you to Holly, Alice, and Nancy for all of your invaluable feedback. Thank you Shannon for signing up this series. And thanks to Angela, Brian, Elias, Emma, Lynsey, Nic, and my mom for pushing me to write!

Eric Huang

Acknowledgements

A big thanks to Kat and Sarah for all of the fantastic design work and steering of the ship on this series. Thank you also Doreen, Kate, and Tom for the opportunity and continued support.

Sam Caldwell

ABOUT THE ILLUSTRATOR

Sam Caldwell is an illustrator based in Glasgow where he lives with his wife and two cats: Tonks and Luna. Sam loves inventing characters and creating images packed full of detail, texture, and color. He is passionate about animals and nature, and when he's not drawing, Sam can often be found exploring the Scottish Highlands. He has illustrated many books for children, including the award-winning *Do Bears Poop In The Woods*?